The Song of Songs
SHIR HASHIRIM

Translated, with an Introduction by
WILLIS BARNSTONE

GREEN INTEGER
KØBENHAVEN & LOS ANGELES
2002

GREEN INTEGER
Edited by Per Bregne
København/Los Angeles

Distributed in the United States by Consortium Book
Sales and Distribution, 1045 Westgate Drive, Suite 90
Saint Paul, Minnesota 55114-1065

(323) 857-1115 / www.greeninteger.com

First Green Integer Edition published in 2002
©1993 by Willis Barnstone
The book was originally published as
The Song of Songs (New York: Sackett & Milk, 1993).
An earlier version appeared as *The Song of Songs: Shir Hashirim*
in a limited edition published by Kedros Publishers in Athens, Greece, 1970.

Cover: *Head of Solomon* [detail] by Pietro Perugino
Design: Douglas Messerli
Typography: Katie Messborn

LIBRARY OF CONGRESS CATALOGING IN PUBLICATION DATA
The Song of Songs
ISBN: 1-931243-05-0
p.cm — Green Integer 76
I.Title II. Series III. Translator

Green Integer books are published for Douglas Messerli
Printed in the United States of America on acid-free paper

for Sarah Handler

CONTENTS

INTRODUCTION

There are poems and there is a poem of poems. *The Song of Songs*, a sequence of Hebrew lyrics from western Asia, has survived for three millennia as the poetic book of books in Israel, Europe and ultimately everywhere. This biblical poem has been given multiple titles and its speakers diverse names; it has suffered many historical interpretations, and its words have been fiddled with—as has been the fate of all biblical texts—by many redacting fingers. Yet despite centuries of intentional miscopying and alterations, the sequence of *The Song of Songs* persists as the most profound and beautiful book of love poems in the world. It is the song of songs.

Like Mirabai's songs to the Dark One or those lyrics that Ezra Pound and Noel Stock rescued from Egyptian hieroglyph or the finding-and-losing poems of Li Po or the lying-alone-in-bed poems of Sappho and Izumi Shikabu, *The Song of Songs* is the quintessential document of love between woman and man, of lovers who search, join in body and spirit, and depart. In *The Song* are the darkness of solitude, the sensual culmination and joy of union, the despair of abandonment, and the morning landscape of reunion. Love as an emotion and state of being is its own end. Love is better than wine, stronger than death. It justifies human existence. *The Song* states itself in images and dramatic passion. It is naked and carries its own complexity. Allusions are secondary and later allegorical readings of a theological and mystical nature are gratuitous, a boon for those who need to invent a reading for their special slant and intent. But the texts as they are, richly impure, reworked by many hungry hands, remain candid, obverse, provocatively obscure, and startlingly wondrous poems of love. Like the greatest poems, they are devoid of certain meaning and continue after the last word, never finished, and demand and invite rereading.

In their single yet cumulative sequence, their simplicity grows deep.

The Song of Songs in its present form appears to be a fragmentary love idyll, with a dramatic structure, albeit a confused one. It is the sole book of love poems in the Bible, and has been the influential book of love lyrics in the West, including Hellenistic Alexandria where the Greek Septuagint version was made and where the poems began their ascent of the mystical stairway. Although the original lyrics have no surface religious meaning, these love poems have been widely interpreted, in both Jewish and Christian traditions, as a spiritual allegory of union with the deity. We read reworkings and interpretations from early Kabbalah to the thirteenth century *Libre d'amic e Amat* (Book of the Friend and the Beloved) by Ramon Llull, the Catalan Illuminated Doctor. *The Song's* strong sensual elements are normally allegorized to diminish the perception of physical lovers and to transform eros into a celebration of a mystical marriage of Israel to Yahweh in the Hebrew Bible and of the church to Christ in the New Covenant. The Spanish poet Saint John of the Cross (1542-91) wrote magnificent mystico-erotic versions of *The Songs of Songs* in his "Spiritual Canticle" and "Dark Night of the Soul" in which his voice is of the female lover. The Carmelite monk poet enters the mist of heresy by ignoring state and church and creating a personal mystical union of a single woman with God.

The Song's title in Hebrew is "the Song of Songs which are of Solomon." We sometimes read the Songs of Solomon or the Canticles. The uncertainty of the title implies large questions of what are the songs, when they were written and by whom. Many books of the Bible have been ascribed to great figures—Moses, David, Solomon, Isaiah, Daniel—whose presumed authorship was at one time sufficient to insure inclusion in the canon. While tradition ascribes *The Song of Songs* to Solomon, the tenth-century B.C.E. king of Israel, the notion is discounted by modern scholars. Some claim the poems to be Hebrew versions of Egyptian popular love songs, and there is certainly an affinity with extant songs surviving from the Late Kingdom period. A common notion is that they are wedding songs, an idea which accommodates religious orthodoxy. We may recall that until mid-century, even classical scholars assumed that Sappho's passionate poems to other women were wedding songs addressed to the bride. In this love poem, the male speaker is a king and the woman a dark handsome woman, maybe a shepherd or goatherd The male figure praises and the female praises, but the woman also longs and suffers. When she searches for her lover, she is stopped and beaten by the city guardians, for whom she has contempt. Their love is in the privacy of their paradise, their enclosed orchards and gardens, and escape into the countryside and small villages. Their love is stronger than jealousy, death, and society.

Lovers are alone and love is their physical and spiritual god of their huge paradise.

No reliable close dating of the text is possible. It is safe to say that these poems were written between the tenth and third centuries B.C.E. It is probable that the poems were composed, by various hands, between the fifth and third centuries and that the variant titles of the collection as well as the names of the main speakers, Solomon and the Shulamite, are contributions of later compilers. The extant Hebrew text offers little help as to when a poem begins and ends and who the speaker is. While there remains a haunting repetition of key passage and choral refrain, even the present dramatic narration is probably the contribution of later editors. With all the tampering and rewriting the work survives as a perfectly intoxicating poetic sequence.

Like other translators of *The Song of Songs*, I have inferred the poem's boundaries and have added titles for purposes of focus and of information. The translation is close and austerely plain. If it has felicities, they exist because this version copies the voice of the Hebrew scripture. I have resisted the trap of "improving" upon *The Song*; and wherever possible have not sought equivalences but to mirror original image and meaning of the Hebrew poem, which, with no need of ornamentation, through time's rags and tattered texts, sings itself.

This version was made from the Masoretic Hebrew text. I also consulted the Septuagint Ἄσμα ᾿σμάτων (Asma Asmáton) and George Seferis's consummate version in Modern Greek. I wish to thank Professor Malcolm Boxer for his collaborative aid in interpreting the Hebrew text and for many evenings spent in checking each sentence of the translation. I wish also to make grateful acknowledgement to Margarita Simontov, Israeli cultural attaché in Athens, for her help in the enigma of alternate meanings.   — *Willis Barnstone*

Your Love Is Better than Wine

Kiss me with kisses from your mouth.
Your love is better than wine.
Your ointments have a good fragrance!
Your name is spread far like fragrance of
    oils
poured on the body
and so young women love you.
Take my hand.
We will run together.

You the king took me to your rooms.
I am happy, happy in you,
and say your love at night is better than
    wine.
It is right for me to love you.

I Am Black

I am black yet beautiful
daughters of Jerusalem,
as black as Kedar's tents,
as lovely as Solomon's tapestries.
Don't look at me with scorn
because I am black,
because the sun has scorched me.

My mother's sons hated me.
They made me guardian of the vineyards
yet I failed to guard my own vineyard.
You whom my soul loves, tell me
where you graze your sheep,
where they lie down at noon.

Why should I wander veiled
among the flocks of your companions?

LIKE MY GLOWING MARE

O beautiful one, if you don't know,
go and follow the flocks
and feed your lambs and small goats
by the shepherd's tents.

I compare you to my mare
glowing among the Pharaoh's stallions.
Your cheeks tease me with earrings,
your neck with strings of jewels.
I will make gold loops for your ears,
with studs of silver.

BETWEEN MY BREASTS

While the king lay on his couch
the spikenard aroma of my body filled the
    air.
My love is a sachet of myrrh
as he lies at night between my breasts.
My love is a cluster of henna blossoms
in the desert orchard of Ein Gedi.

KING AND WOMAN

You are beautiful, my darling.
You are beautiful,
your eyes are doves.

You are beautiful, my lover.
You are beautiful,
our couch is the fresh grass,
the beams of our house are cedar,
our rafters are the cypress.

Rose

I am a rose of Sharon,
a lily of the valleys.

Lily

A lily among thorns
is my love among women.

IN THE ROOMS

An apple tree among young men.
I delight in his shadow

and lie before him
and his fruit is sweet to my tongue.

He led me to his drinking room
and his banner over me is love.

Feed me your raisins,
comfort me with apples,

for I am sick with love.
His left hand is under my head,

his right hand caresses my body.
O daughters of Jerusalem,

swear by the gazelles
and the deer of the hills

not to wake us
till after we have merged in love.

MY LOVER'S VOICE

My lover's voice is coming.
Hear him. O hear

him leaping on the mountains,
dancing on the hills!

My love is like a gazelle
or a young stag.

Here he is standing
behind our wall,

gazing in through the window,
peering through the lattice.

My lover answers
and speaks to me:

"Rise, my love, my beauty
and come away.

Winter is past,
the rains are over and gone.

Wild flowers appear on the earth,
the time of the nightingale has come.

The voice of the turtledove
is heard in our land.

The fig tree is grown heavy
with small green figs,

and grapevines are in bloom,
pouring out fragrance.

Rise, my love, my beauty,
and come away.

My dove, you are in the crevices of the
    rock,
in the recess of the cliffs.

Let me look at your face,
let me hear you.

Your voice is delicious
and your face is clear beauty."

The Foxes

We must catch the foxes,
the little foxes,

who are ravaging the grapes.
Our vineyards are in blossom.

In Lilies and Mountains

My lover is mine
and I am his.

He feeds his sheep
among the lilies.

Till day cools
and shadows tumble,

come stay with me.
Be a gazelle

or a young stag bounding
on jagged mountains.

In My Bed at Night

In my bed at night
I look for him whom my soul loves
and cannot find him.

I'll rise and wander in the city
through streets and markets,
looking for him whom my soul loves.

Yet I cannot find him.
The watchmen who go about the city
find me. I ask them:

Have you seen him whom my soul loves?
I barely leave them
when I find him whom my soul loves.

I seize him. I won't let him go
until I've taken him to my mother's room
and he is lying in the bed

of her who conceived me.
O daughters of Jerusalem,
swear by the gazelles

and the deer of the hills
not to wake us
till after we have merged in love.

SOLOMON IS COMING

Who is coming up from the sand and
                        wilderness
   like a pillar of smoke
   from burning myrrh and frankincense
   and all the powders of the merchant?

Look. It is the carriage of Solomon
   and around it sixty brave men,
   sixty brave men from Israel.
      They carry swords and are expert in war.

Swords are strapped to their thighs
   against the terror in the night.
   King Solomon made a carriage
   from the cedars of Lebanon.

He made the posts of silver, its backs
   of gold, its seat purple
and the interior inlaid with love
   by the daughters of Jerusalem.

Come outdoors, daughters of Zion. Gaze
   on the king with the crown
his mother gave him on his wedding day,
   the day his heart was happy.

YOUR LIPS ARE A THREAD OF SCARLET

You are beauty, my love,
you are the beautiful.
Your eyes are doves

behind your veil.
Your hair is a flock
of black goats weaving

down the hills of Gilead.
Your teeth are flocks
of lambs newly shorn

fresh from the watering
trough, perfect,
with no flaw in them.

Your lips are a thread
of scarlet and your voice
is cloth of softness.

Your cheeks are halves
of a fresh pomegranate
cut open and gleaming

behind your veil.
Your neck is a straight
tower of David

built with turrets
and a thousand shields,
armor of brave men.

Your breasts are twin
fawns, twins of a gazelle
feeding among the lilies.

BEFORE TWILIGHT

Till afternoon is cold
and its shadows blur,

I will climb over
the mountains of myrrh

and wander across a hill
of spices.

PERFECTION

In you is beauty,
my lover, with
no stain in you.

Come Away with Me

Come away with me. Let us leave
   Lebanon.
Let us leave the hills,
my bride,
Come down from the peak of Amana.
Let us descend the peaks of Senir
and Hermon. We will abandon
the dens of lions
and walk down the mountain of leopards.

LOVE BETTER THAN WINE

You have ravished my heart, my sister,
 my bride,
you ravished my heart with one of your
 eyes,
with a single jewel from your necklace.
How tasty are your breasts, my sister,
 my bride!
How much better is your love than wine.
Your ointments are richer than any spice,
your lips drip like the honeycomb,
 my bride,
and under your tongue are honey and milk.
Your clothing tastes of Lebanon's
 meadows.

My Sister, My Bride

My sister, my bride, you are a garden
enclosed and hidden,

a spring locked up, a fountain sealed.
Your cheeks

are an orchard of pomegranates
with rare fruits,

henna, spikenard, spikenard and saffron,
calamus and cinnamon

and every tree bearing incense. From you
drip aloes

and all choice spices. You are a fountain
of gardens,

a well of living waters and bubbling springs
from Lebanon.

"an orchard of pomegranates." In 4:13 Hebrew
parades, "paradise," is a loan word from Persian and
the phrase could read "a paradise of pomegranates."

WINDS

Awake, north wind and come, south wind!
Blow on my garden, let the spices

be tossed about. Let my love come into
his garden and eat his precious fruits.

GARDENER

My sister and bride, I enter the orchard
  and gather wild herbs and condiments.
I eat my honeycomb with honey, drink
  wine with milk.

Friends and lovers, imitate me. Drink deep.

MY HAIR IS WET WITH DROPS OF NIGHT

I'm sleeping but my heart is awake.
My lover's voice is knocking:
"Open, let me in, my sister and darling,
    my dove and perfect one
My head is soaked with dew,
my hair is wet with drops of night."

I have taken off my garments.
How can I put them on?
I have washed my feet.
How can I dirty them now?
My lover's hand shows at the door
and in me I burn for him.
I rise to open to my love,
my hands drip with liquid myrrh,
my fingers drench perfume
over the handle of the bolt.
I open to my love
but my love has turned and gone.
He has vanished.

When he spoke my soul vanished.
I look for him and can't find him.
I call. He doesn't answer.
The watchmen who go about the city
find me.
They beat me, they wound me,
they strip me of my mantle,
those guardians of the walls!

I beg you, daughters of Jerusalem,
if you find my love
you will say
that I am sick with love.

Her Companions

How is your friend the prince of lovers,
O beautiful woman?
How is your friend the prince of lovers?
Why do you swear us to an oath?

Doves by the Small Rivers

My love is radiant. He is ruddy,
one in ten thousand.
His head is fine gold,
his locks are palm leaves in the wind,
black like ravens.
His eyes are doves by the small rivers.
They are bathed in milk
and deeply set.
His cheeks are a bed of spices
blowing in fragrance.
His lips are lilies,
moist with tastes.
His arms are rounded gold
inset with beryl.
His belly is luminous ivory
starred with sapphires.
His legs are columns of alabaster
set on bases of gold.

His appearance is the tall city of Lebanon,
excellent with cedars.
His mouth is luscious, made of desire,
all of him is pleasant.
This is my lover and friend,
O daughters of Jerusalem.

COMPANIONS

Where has your lover gone, beautiful
    woman?
He's disappeared. Where has he turned to?
Tell us. We will help you find him.

LILIES

My love has gone down to his garden
to the beds of spices,
to feed his sheep in the orchards,
to gather lilies.
I am my lover's and my lover is mine.
He feeds his flock among the lilies.

A City with Banners

Your beauty is of Tirzah
or even Jerusalem
and frightening as

an army with banners.
Look away from me.
You make me tremble.

You hair is a flock
of black goats weaving
down the hills of Gilead.

Your teeth are flocks
of lambs newly shorn
fresh from the watering

trough, perfect,
with no flaw in them.
Your cheeks are halves

of a fresh pomegranate
cut open and gleaming
behind your veil.

Sixty queens and eighty
concubines and countless
virgins are nothing

like my dove, my perfect
love who is unique. She's
the darling of her mother.

Women look at her and call
her happy. Concubines
and queens praise her.

Who is she? Her gaze
is daybreak, her beauty
the moon, and she is

the transparent sun,
yet frightening as
an army with banners.

WALKING AROUND

I go down to the orchard of nut trees
to see the green plants of the valley,
to see if the vines are in bud,
whether the pomegranates have
    blossomed.
Unaware, my soul leads me
into a chariot beside my prince.

COME BACK

Come back, come back, O Shulamite,
and we shall look at you.

DANCER

Will you look at the Shulamite
as at a dancer before two armies?

YOUR NAVEL A MOON-HOLLOW GOBLET

Your sandaled feet define grace,
O queenly woman!

Your round thighs are jewels,
handiwork of a cunning craftsman,

your navel a moon-hollow goblet
filled with mixed wines.

Your belly is a bed of wheat
laced with daffodils.

Your two breasts are two fawns,
twins of a gazelle.

Your neck is a tower of ivory,
your eyes are pools in Heshbon

by the gate of Beth-rabbim.
Your nose is a tower of Lebanon

facing the city of Damascus.
Your head is like Carmel,

and purple is your flowing hair
in which a king lies captive.

How calm and beautiful you are,
my happy love.

You are stately like a palm tree
and your breasts a cluster of grapes.

I Will Climb

I will climb the palm tree
and take hold of the bough.
Let your breasts be the grapes of the vine,
your breath the taste of apples.
Your mouth is choice wine,
and swallowing it smoothly
makes my lips tremble in sleep.

LET US GO OUT INTO THE FIELDS

I am my lover's and he desires me.

Come, my darling,
let us go out into the fields
and spend the night in villages.
Let us wake early and go to the vineyards
and see if the vine is in blossom,
if the new grapebud is open
and the pomegranates are in bloom.

There I will give you my love.
The mandrakes will spray aroma,
and over our door will be precious fruit,
all the new and old
that I have saved for you, my darling.

IF YOU WERE MY BROTHER

Oh, if you were my brother
who sucked my mother's breasts!

When I find you in the streets
or country, unashamed

I will kiss you
and no one will despise me.

I'll take you to my mother's home
and into her room

where she conceived me
and there you'll instruct me.

I'll give you spiced wine to drink,
the juice of my pomegranates.

Your left hand lies under my head,
your right hand caresses my body.

O daughters of Jerusalem,
swear by the deer of the hills

not to wake us
till after we have merged in love.

COMPANIONS

Who is coming out of the desert
   wilderness,
leaning on her lover?

UNDER THE APPLE TREE

Under the apple tree I aroused you
and you woke to me
where your mother was in labor,
where she who bore you was in labor.

A Seal on Your Heart

Set me as a seal on your heart,
as a seal on your arm,
for love is strong as death.
Jealousy is cruel as the grave.
Its flashes are flashes of fire,
a flame of God.
Many waters cannot quench love,
rivers cannot drown it.
If a man measured love
by all the wealth of his house,
he would be utterly scorned.

THE BROTHERS

We have a young sister
and she has no breasts.
What will we do for our sister
when they ask for her hand?
If she is a wall
we will build turrets of silver on her.
If she is a door
we will enclose her with boards of cedar.

HER TOWERS

I am a wall
and my breasts are towers,
and in his eyes
I bring peace.

HER VINEYARD

Solomon has a vineyard at Baal-hamon.
He let out the vines to the guardians,
each bringing a thousand pieces of silver
for the good fruit.

My own vineyard is about me.
You may keep the thousand, my king,
and use two hundred to pay off the
    guardians.

THE KING BEGS

You who live in the gardens,
my friends are listening for your voice.
Let me hear it too.

COME, YOUNG STAG

Hurry, my darling!
and be like a gazelle
or a young stag
upon my mountain of spices.

GREEN INTEGER
Pataphysics and Pedantry

Edited by Per Bregne
Douglas Messerli, *Publisher*

Essays, Manifestos, Statements, Speeches,
Maxims, Epistles, Diaristic Notes,
Narratives, Natural Histories, Poems,
Plays, Performances, Ramblings,
Revelations and all such ephemera
as may appear necessary to
bring society into a slight tremolo
of confusion and fright
at least.

*

Published books

History, or Messages from History
Gertrude Stein [1997]
Notes on the Cinematographer Robert Bresson
[1997]
The Critic As Artist Oscar Wilde [1997]
Tent Posts Henri Michaux [1997]
Eureka Edgar Allan Poe [1997]
An Interview Jean Renoir [1997]
Mirrors Marcel Cohen [1998]